Little People, **BIG DREAMS**

VIVIENNE WESTWOOD

Written by
Mª Isabel Sánchez Vegara

Illustrated by
Laura Callaghan

Frances Lincoln
Children's Books

Little Vivienne lived in a little town called Tintwistle, in England. She was born during a great world war, and while her mom darned her socks, she dreamed of mending the world.

At school, there was a boy all the children bullied—
they called him "Dirty Edward." But Vivienne didn't. She
always stood up for the outsiders: she told everyone
she was his girlfriend, even though it wasn't true.

When Vivienne was older, her family moved to the outskirts of London. Vivienne was always curious about art and new ideas, so she decided to study fashion and jewelry design.

Making a living as an artist was difficult, so Vivienne pursued a career in teaching. She liked being a teacher, but her head and heart were elsewhere…

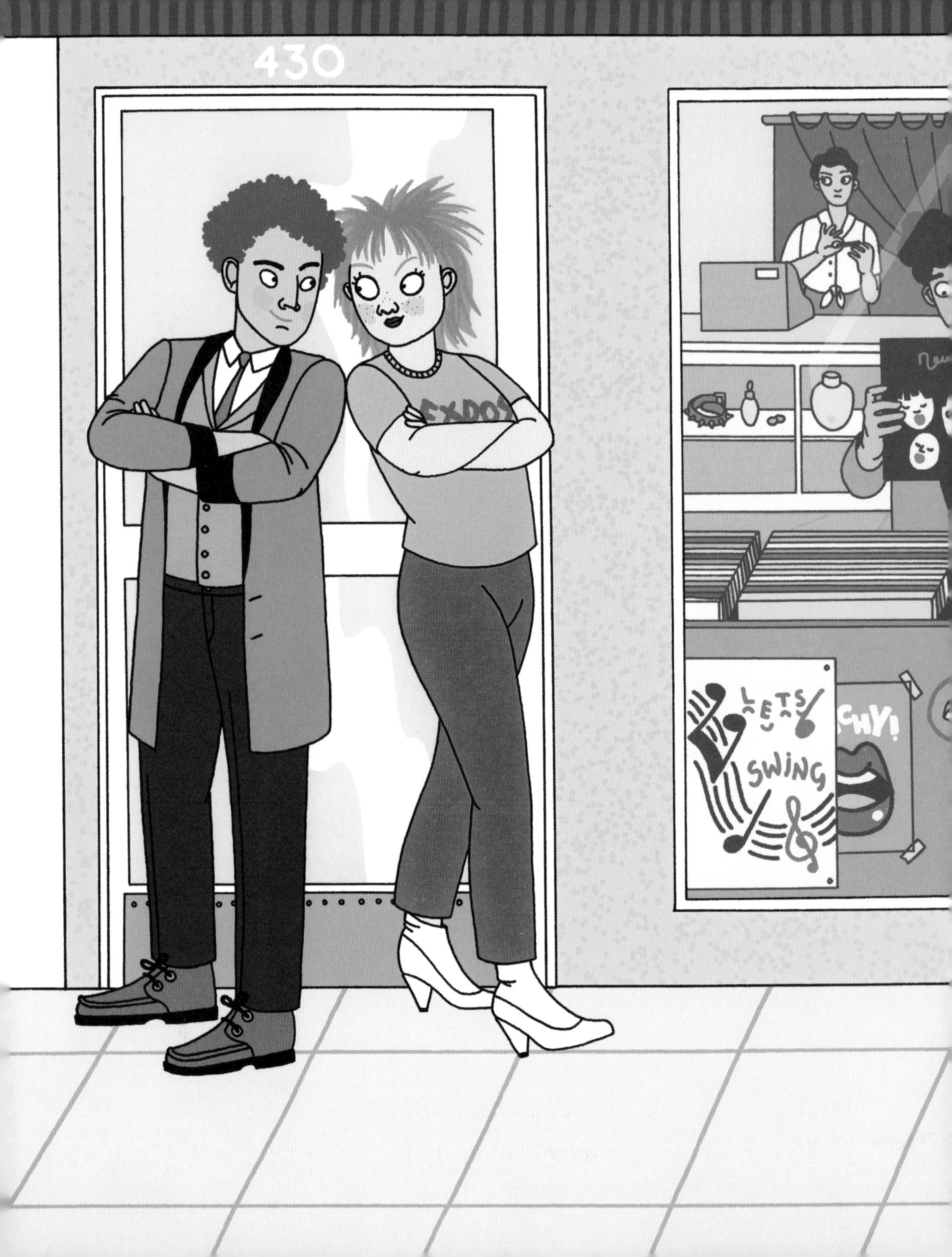
430
LETS
SWING

One day, she met a rebellious young man named Malcolm McLaren. They opened a shop on the King's Road in London, where they mixed rock 'n' roll records with fashion in a brand-new way.

Vivienne took apart old clothes from the 1950s to create new designs. She started ripping the garments before threading them with safety pins and writing shocking statements on every T-shirt.

Clothes became her way to speak out and protest. Bands took notice, and soon, she was dressing musicians with chains and collars. Her style was as loud and chaotic as the new sound in town: punk.

With their next collection, Vivienne and Malcolm sailed away from King's Road and docked on the catwalk.

They plundered ideas from the past and dressed models as pirates and buccaneers. It was an anti-fashion revolution!

After years together, Vivienne felt it was time to go her own way and said goodbye to Malcolm. She was about to change the shape of women's clothes, with her corsets and bubble skirts.

Many critics found Vivienne's clothes unwearable, but she was not interested in their opinions. She would much rather read a good book than any fashion magazine.

Vivienne mixed punk and aristocracy, making the poor look rich and the rich look poor. She dressed artists, actresses, and even some members of royalty.

Vivienne became an activist against climate change.
She made quality clothes that were built to last,
encouraging people to buy less and wear them more.

And little Vivienne, who always stood up for the outsiders, became the most unique and outspoken fashion designer, ever.

All because she believes that those
who dare to speak up can change the world.

VIVIENNE WESTWOOD

(Born 1941)

1977

1982

Vivienne Westwood is one of the most famous and outspoken fashion designers in the world. She was born in the north of England, to a family with a long history of shoemaking—but there were no other signs of the future fashion icon Vivienne would grow to become. When she was 17, her family moved to Harrow, on the outskirts of London. There, she worked at a local factory and trained to be a teacher, while making jewelry on the side—selling it at a little stall on Portobello Road in London. However, her life changed when she met a man named Malcolm McLaren. She was suddenly introduced to a world of art, politics, and freedom. Together, they opened a clothes shop at number 430 King's Road in London. Vivienne designed clothes for sale, emblazoning T-shirts with shocking statements, ripping up fabric, and using everyday objects, like safety pins, as decoration.

2000   2003

She created a new style, based on being nonconformist. Their shop became an important place for the punk movement in the 1970s—and Vivienne clothed the most famous punk bands of the time. Vivienne eventually left Malcolm and established her own identity as a fashion designer. She created a fashion empire, with key pieces that revolutionized traditional fabrics and styles, like tartan, tweed, crinoline, corsets, and knitwear. Vivienne is also a passionate climate change activist, believing that fashion can make a difference in the world. Her motto is to "buy less, choose well, and make it last." In 2006, she was made Dame Commander of the Order of the British Empire (DBE) and has since been described as "the Coco Chanel of our day." She now designs clothes to make people feel "grand and strong," whoever they are.

Want to find out more about **Vivienne Westwood?**
Read this great book:

Vogue on Vivienne Westwood (Vogue on Designers) by Linda Watson

You can also browse the V&A Museum online, to view some of Vivienne's collections.

BOARD BOOKS

COCO CHANEL

ISBN: 978-1-78603-245-4

MAYA ANGELOU

ISBN: 978-1-78603-249-2

FRIDA KAHLO

ISBN: 978-1-78603-247-8

AMELIA EARHART

ISBN: 978-1-78603-252-2

MARIE CURIE

ISBN: 978-1-78603-253-9

ADA LOVELACE

ISBN:978-1-78603-259-1

ROSA PARKS

ISBN: 978-1-78603-263-8

EMMELINE PANKHURST

ISBN: 978-1-78603-261-4

AUDREY HEPBURN

ISBN: 978-1-78603-255-3

ELLA FITZGERALD

ISBN:978-1-78603-257-7

BOOKS & PAPER DOLLS

EMMELINE PANKHURST

ISBN: 978-1-78603-400-7

MARIE CURIE

ISBN: 978-1-78603-401-4

BOX SETS

WOMEN IN ART

ISBN: 978-1-78603-428-1

WOMEN IN SCIENCE

ISBN: 978-1-78603-429-8

Collect the
Little People,
BIG DREAMS
series:

FRIDA KAHLO

ISBN: 978-1-84780-783-0

COCO CHANEL
ISBN: 978-1-84780-784-7

MAYA ANGELOU

ISBN: 978-1-84780-889-9

AMELIA EARHART

ISBN: 978-1-84780-888-2

AGATHA CHRISTIE

ISBN: 978-1-84780-960-5

MARIE CURIE

ISBN: 978-1-84780-962-9

ROSA PARKS

ISBN: 978-1-78603-018-4

AUDREY HEPBURN

ISBN: 978-1-78603-053-5

EMMELINE PANKHURST
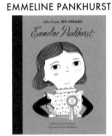
ISBN: 978-1-78603-020-7

ELLA FITZGERALD
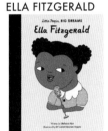
ISBN: 978-1-78603-087-0

ADA LOVELACE

ISBN: 978-1-78603-076-4

JANE AUSTEN
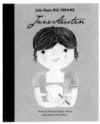
ISBN: 978-1-78603-120-4

GEORGIA O'KEEFFE

ISBN: 978-1-78603-122-8

HARRIET TUBMAN
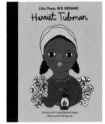
ISBN: 978-1-78603-227-0

ANNE FRANK

ISBN: 978-1-78603-229-4

MOTHER TERESA

ISBN: 978-1-78603-230-0

JOSEPHINE BAKER

ISBN: 978-1-78603-228-7

L. M. MONTGOMERY

ISBN: 978-1-78603-233-1

JANE GOODALL

ISBN: 978-1-78603-231-7

SIMONE DE BEAUVOIR

ISBN: 978-1-78603-232-4

MUHAMMAD ALI
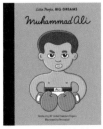
ISBN: 978-1-78603-331-4

STEPHEN HAWKING

ISBN: 978-1-78603-333-8

MARIA MONTESSORI

ISBN: 978-1-78603-755-8

VIVIENNE WESTWOOD

ISBN: 978-1-78603-757-2

Brimming with creative inspiration, how-to projects, and useful information to enrich your everyday life, Quarto Knows is a favorite destination for those pursuing their interests and passions. Visit our site and dig deeper with our books into your area of interest: Quarto Creates, Quarto Cooks, Quarto Homes, Quarto Lives, Quarto Drives, Quarto Explores, Quarto Gifts, or Quarto Kids.

First Published in the UK in 2019 by Frances Lincoln Children's Books, an imprint of The Quarto Group.

400 First Avenue North, Suite 400, Minneapolis, MN 55401, USA.

T (612) 344-8100 F (612) 344-8692 **www.QuartoKnows.com**

First Published in Spain in 2019 under the title Pequeña & Grande Vivienne Westwood

by Alba Editorial, s.l.u., Baixada de Sant Miquel, 1, 08002 Barcelona

www.albaeditorial.es

ISBN 978-1-78603-757-2

The illustrations were created with watercolor, India ink, and isograph pen.

Set in Futura BT.

Published by Rachel Williams • Designed by Karissa Santos

Edited by Katy Flint • Production by Jenny Cundill

Manufactured in Guangdong, China CC122018

9 7 5 3 1 2 4 6 8

Photographic acknowledgements (pages 28–29, from left to right) 1. Vivienne Westwood, 1977 © Hulton Archive / Peter Cade via Getty Images 2. Vivienne Westwood, 1982 © Hulton Archive / Michael Putland via Getty Images 3. Vivienne Westwood, 2000 © Archive photos / Rose Hartman via Getty Images 4. Vivienne Westwood, 2003 © Hulton Archive / Polly Borland via Getty Images.